Priscilla's Smile

By J. Bridgers

Priscilla's Smile

By Josephine J. Bridgers

copyright 2011

All Rights Reserved. No part of this book should be transmitted or reproduced by means of: electronic, mechanic, this includes photocopying, recording or any information storage and retrieval system without the permission from the copyright owner, Josephine Jenkins Bridgers

(Book Cover design for Priscilla's Smile by Denise Sharpe)

Imprint: Jan'na HCS

Jealousy

Blinds a person

from their potential

Some people have reached out and touched love

But it eluded them to a chase but I am blessed beyond words because everyday I wake up and see

Calvin's face

In you I see me

In you they see a bald head, eyes with bags
In me they see, a flat rear end and a thinning hairline
But what I see in you, I see a handsome man
Bags maybe, but filled with presents of little what nots from   years of loving me
But in me they see thicknesss, bulges shielded my hips; "you can pinch more than a inch." My hair you see a silver lining filled with years, of you loving me and me loving you
Even though the world see a mortal man, I see a prince and I'm his princess.
On our first romantic vacation, I watched from the window as he walked proudly back up the stairs, seeing me his eyes ignited a sparkle, as if I was his one and only and he had been blessed with a prize. Eyes blinded by beauty, the day time recaptured our youth and there glazing back in the mirror, two youthful beauties stood.
No bags, hair glossy and to our amazement, rejuvenated behinds!
Through the years, we've grown into each other's skin. In him I see me, a timeless love that has shattered the hourglass of time.

In You I See Me is dedicated to my Husband, Calvin Bridgers. He doesn't ask for much, but love me 100%

Table of Content

Love that couldn't speak..................................13

My Darling Black Rose................................15

Tribute page 17

Love Don't Pay the Bills............................19

Portrayal of Love......................................22

On the Wings of an Angel........................ 25

Celbrating my Daughter Birthday................ 26

Timeless Love... 28

Sweet Lulby... .30

Fatherless..32

Little Lost Child.......................................33

The Unopened Present............................36

You don't Love me.................................37

Invincible...39

Grown Folk Love...................................40

Pressing On...44

Time..46
  No Regrets..49
  Change..51
  I am a Man..52
  Successful Failure..54
  Mr. Freeze..55
  What a Child Needs..56
  Fragment..58
   Repercusions...60
In the Midst of Darkness.......................................61
Being in Love..64
Heir...67
  I Remember..68
Ghetto Language..70
The Essence of Fear..72
Helpless...73
Who Are You..74
Pricless Memories..75
What Counts..76
I'll be There..77

True Lies	78
Senseless	79
Probably	80
Taste and See	81
Progress On	82
Love Found	83
Respect	84
The Eyes of the Warrior	85
Being in Love	87
Web of Lies	88
Wisom	90
To Know	91
No Cure	95
The Road to Riches	97
Wasted Years	99
Upringing	100
One Way	103
Sins of This World	104
I, You and They	106
Me Against Me	107

Lone Wolf……………………………………………..110

Real…………………………………………………..111

Me and You……………………………………………112

Lovers of the Flesh…………………………………..116

A Mother Plead to her Child to be Strong…………117

To live in Peace………………………………………119

Love Doesn't Happen by Chance………………......120

What does the Word Friend Means?…………………121

Africa I Hear Your Cry……………………………......124

A boy Named Nigger…………………………………126

Paying my Dues………………………………………130

Author Insight about being Black…………………..134

Black Man……………………………………………..137

An Angel in Waiting…………………………………..139

No Regret (JJB) ……………………………………...143

Game Changing………………………………………145

Envision Rosa Parks…………………………………149

Priscilla's Smile

Priscilla's Smile is a tribute to the author's niece who is battling stomach cancer

Priscillia's Smile is a revision of Memento but with a soulful twist of words as the author takes you on a journey that will leave you speechless.

Priscilla's Smille is a collection of poems selected to speak to the audience in a way that words can' t articulate.

These poets in this collection walk you on a expedition using their imaginations and their experiences.

This book represents different genres but has a common goal, which is to excite your critical thinking.

Whether you are experiencing joy or sadness,

Priscilla' s Smile will plant a smile on your face. The author's guide is movtivated by these themes: A time to Live, a time to die, a time to be happy, and a time to be sad.

Also, thanks to Jamey Wilkins co-author in this collection for his contribution.

Additionally, I would like to thank the Allegra family located in Rocky Mount NC for their assistance.

If we were only color blind, we wouldn't see color as a challenge

A love that couldn't speak by JJB

Exquisite daisies draped in pinstriped ribbons

Symbolizing diaries of love fashioned in the flowery breeze

Why is going the distance so unbearable to the unwise?

Have the dust blanketed my chest into a mountainous plain

Diced with melons and cherries

Still I pondered as I sat scrutinizing the flowers as they saluted their buds in the hot, humid summer heat

There was an ancient time when snow and ice teased my lips for only a second prompting me to smile

But my thoughts were interrupted, when I unepectantly saw a dog hobbling along with a squirrel

These picturesque bubbles of love, ride on the notes of a song

Notes that elevate me

High in the clouds

Unspoiled, these timeless moments when the rhythm of my

chest is rejuvenated by the sting of a bumble bee. Then out of a misty blue day, my forgotten love shows his face

His body invokes his power over me that seemed to be hidden behind years of broken dreams

Slowly, slowly

He turns

Exposing his tears

Tears I welcomed like a friend

Then he reached out with his outstretched hands

His eyes told the love story

That his voice couldn't speak

I love you he whispered

My Darling Black Rose by Matthew Jenkins Jr.

O how fragile your petals, green stalk

burdened with thorns. How

unfortunate your beauty, for it goes

untouched, my darling black Rose.

Please see what I see. Your worth and

beauty resonate exponentially for

those blessed to be in your presence.

Saccharine Sweet Sad Black Rose.

Allow time to melt away the painful

reminiscence of thorns so sharp they

pierced your supple skin and extended

beyond your deepest self; schemingly

placed so that not only are you

protected, but your present yourself as a

threat to the very word love. Please

be healed, my Black Rose. O how fragile your

petals, green stalk burdened with

thorns. How unfortunate your beauty,

for it goes untouched, for no one

knows the pain that resides within

you. Allow the warm light of love to

help you grow for the special day you

are embraced, My Black Rose

Tribute page

Priscilla's Smile is a tribute to the author's niece, Priscilla. Priscilla is battling the fight of her life, stomach cancer. After discovering this, the author decided to revise her poetry book, Mementos, to Priscilla's Smile.

Priscilla's Smile incorporates all these rhymesters' thoughts and journeys with a soulful twist evoking emotions and rejuvenating their spirits.

This journey walks you along with Priscilla while she fights aggressively to beat this illness that has claimed so many lives.

Priscilla's smile is a dedication to all the people dealing with cancer and the aftermath that has left so many casualties blindsided and devastated. It is the author's hope that this book will help heal their wounds and plant a smile on their face.

A smile shouldn't be taken for granted.; smiling is therapeutic; it is nature's way of healing the soul.

The author will take you along on a pleasurable escapade and hope you will be able to retrace the times when living and dreaming is a commodity and not a task.

The poets in this amazing collection, tell their stories relying on their own experiences and their aspirations.

Priscilla's Smile is a motivation piece for those yearning to be heard but can't articulate their own words.

Composition of Priscilla's Smile, the author enlisted family members for this book to complete her vision.

The author believes that life holds many treasures; she believes that if we stand on its foundation, we will cultivate our gift by watering it, vocally or by the written words.

Sometimes in life we hold on to things that are less important instead of supporting each other when a friend is needed, or a listening ear is required.

Let's walk along with Priscilla's Smile while she fight a heartfelt fight to beat this devastating illness by praying for her recovery and extending words of comfort....

Love don't pay the bill by JJB

Poppy tails and centerpieces

I'm in love with my boo

He's the spirit of my sleep

The nucleus of every word I speak

Sunrise,

Sunset,

Hugging and kissing,

He's my sweet spirit of the streets

I'm too pretty to lift a broom

Nah, no books or education will suit my needs

Love is the main element of my hopes and dreams

You think I s'pose to work when I got my boo

Boom! The bubble burst (loud noise heard)

Giggling and laughing she suddenly stops

I'm having a baby, what am I to do?

I'm just a child

No job

No education

My boo is gone!

Invisible man is he

Fragrance of loveliness

consumes the air

Skyscraping the sky with vanilla wafers as pies

Little tales of dreams he told me

Butterflies

Cotton candy

Tales only one could dream

Looking down, the reality serves as a wake-up call

A new life grows inside of me

Where is my boo now?

Then I remembered

What my momma said, "Child,

'Love don't pay the bill"

Why speak when the truth is not
A priority

Portrait of Love by JJB

Love is intangible, it's something that Can't be touched, but it can be felt. Love has no fragrance, but what makes it unique is, it's a symphony that can't be heard. If love don't hurt, why are so many sad? Is it because it evokes an indescribable feeling that can neither be expressed with tears or pearls? Love is tremendous. Even though some people think it can be bought, love brings out the beauty. But for others, love is a prey of thought. The predator or the prey, it depends on the person seeking to retrieve it. For the selfish ones, they embraced it with empty words. Causing heartaches, an undescribable feeling that evokes many to cry. But few will ever obtain this luxury, because this adjective stands alone taunting people to pursuit it, while others just run away just to avoid the game hidden behind the thorns. But I view love as a portrait, it's invisible like a windstorm that gathers its strength from the blows of the dirt. Love has a taste of uncertainity And yet for me, it is a mastering task just like a portrait encased in a frame not **meant to be claimed.**

On the Wings of an Angel written by Brittany A. Hill

Though your tears may flow

As you experience

A pain no one can ever know

Take the time to cherish the memories

And let love ease your mind

Embrace the footsteps of this ended legacy

And come to know your identity, fulfill your purpose

And live in love, relieve your heavy heart

And rejoice in the start of her heaven sent rewards

As she rejoices among angels

May your tears cease and you no longer wail

Be uplifted and remember

She's on the wings of an angel

Celebrating my daughter Birthday written by Jamey Wilkins

Almost missed it

How would I?

Shocked

As I looked

Into the face of my watch, 5-26

All other thoughts

All other things

Immediately

Ceased to exist

A smile

A tear

Another year

Another month

Another minute

Of her life

Has passed

Without me in it

No letter

No Card

No call

She received

Nothing

That acknowledges

What she achieved

Wishes ungranted

Dreams shattered

Does it matter?

Nope

Because she

Won't get

A thing from me

still….

I remembered

A timely love written by Jamey Wilkins

Yesterday ended when today began

Tomorrow comes when today ends

Time started as soon as I was born

Forever seemed so far away

Eternity will start as soon as I'm gone

And tomorrow will always be today

Yesterday I fell in love with you

And tomorrow I will still be

Cause today I made a vow to love you until eternity

Forever is not long enough

Cause it ends as soon as I die

So until forever comes I want only you in my life

You meant the world to me yesterday

But today you mean much more

By the time tomorrow comes, I will love you even more than before

I promise this through eternity, cause the only way I will depart, is when the day comes you decide to break my heart

Don't ever leave me

Sweet Lullaby Take me Home written by JJB

When I get old and my hair turns grey

Think about all the wisdom that lies beneath each root

When my body seems to ache with every twist and turn.

Don't hurry me away! My bones are brittle, my joints are stiff.

When I sat nodding in my chair, recite a verse in the Bible

To let me know you still care. When the cataracts have made my eyes cloudy, dim the lights,

So I can dream of a life filled with colors with dainty flowers everywhere.

When my legs get flimsy and I can't make it up the stairs, be

the shoulder that I can lean on, be the knight in my corner,

the shield behind the glass

When the darkness covers my sight, pat me on the head my dear child to

let me know everything is alright. When I lie down and

breathe my last breath, don't be sad.

I'm happy; there is no more pain, no hurting or crying, no more shedding tears so don't cry any more tears.

Sweet lullaby, sweet lullaby, take me home

COM' here my beloved daughter, sing me a sweet lullaby

So I can skip, hop, I'm finally going home.

Fatherless written by Jamey Wilkins

As I sit and watch how others play

I wonder if I would be different

Would I be the same, would I see the same

If my father wasn't missing

Would his presence inspire me

Would he guide me, mold me and school me

Would I be better off or would I be worse

What if he beat and abused me

What if he drank all day? Then cursed me out at night

Would I have followed his steps?

And been an alcoholic the rest of my life

Maybe I'm better without one

Still if I had one I wouldn't let him go

Cause maybe he'd simply love me

But I didn't have a father so I'll never know

The Little Lost Girl by JJB

The time is not known

The hours are not yet born

The someplace is hidden from a child

cuddling a warm blanket

Why is the life of a child limited to a person

imagination?

Then out of shame and fear, the little lost

child speaks, she says

"I am only one but to a child of few I am a

little lost girl

I am not defiant in the early stages of my life

Why are my instincts restricted to only my

mother's face?

I am but one, a child, little but lost

A child in quest for the embracement of her

mother's arms

A child that will never see the wrinkles in her

father's face

Or hear the loudness of his voice

But after all I am a little lost girl

I have no ponytails, only a single braid, silky

black that rest

Down my small narrow head

My sisters and brothers are asleep but

thoughts of play are

interrupted by the sounds erupting from my

mother's room

I am quiet, as I escape to a pleasurable time,

where there are

no interruptions, no delays but where a little

lost girl

Can go

Can laugh

Can be reborn

Where a child has a momma, papa and siblings; and has the highest regards for life and love."

As she sits in the corner, quietly, she falls to sleep.

The Unopened Present written by Jamey Wilkins

All I ever wanted was to make momma proud

That's all

And my purpose in life would be fulfilled

But the task has proven harder than expected

Where I thought I was strong my weaknesses were revealed

Intentions were the best

So inside I am at peace

Irregardless what is depicted by the outer?

I tried, but I failed

So my words went unheard

Because my actions always seemed to speak louder

You don't Love me written by Brittany Anjanet Hill

I'm afraid to love you because you might hurt

me

I'm afraid to hate you because I need you

Confused by my emotions

Mislead by your fake devotion

What did I do so wrong for you to hate me?

In a sense you took away my identity by

denying your responsibility.

Time and time you let me down by never

even coming around.

All my life I've wanted your love. You've

denied me endless times.

Your unconditional love, I still can't find. My

tears are falling because

I can't hate you. How can I love you inspite

of everything u do?

Now I'm stronger and I've taken away your

power. Because from you,

I reclaimed my identity

Invincible written by Jamey Wilkins

I don't know defeat, and chances are we will never meet.

My enemies cheat; because that is the only way they can compete.

I've got goals and with God's guide they will be completed.

I want to help those who have been denied and mistreated.

I look for loyalty in all that I know,

A friend is a friend, a foe is a foe. Stay

Close to the strong and outgrow the weak.

I know right, I know wrong, but I don't know Defeat!

Grown Folk Love written by Jamey Wilkins

Sun kissed

Tan, Brown, Ebony, Bronze

In my arms forever

Is where you belong

Eyes like bottomless pits

So deep

Skin chocolaty rich

So sweet

My hand in your hand

Your hand in mine

Skipping along barefoot

Through the sands of time

Chasing the fading sun

Until we are deceased

Knowing you made it safely

Is the only way I'll rest in peace

When I placed you before me

I knew what it was

More than just infatuation

This is Grown Folk Love

Sun kissed

Bronze, Tan, Brown, Ebony

Only God can create

A bond so heavenly

Your hair

Though not the longest

Is still without a doubt

The strongest

Your rib is my rib

My rib is yours

In you I found peace

After so many wars

Your touch alone

Can ease my storms

Whether a peck on the cheek

Or just a squeeze on my arm

Ever since that first time

I knew what it was

This aint no play-play stuff

Naw, this Grown Folk Love

Sun kissed

Ebony, Bronze, Tan, Brown

A smile creases my face

Whenever you come' round

A blessing

Our connection

Is a reflection

Of perfection

I'm your Adam

You're my Eve

On cruise control

You're my speed

No mile

Can separate us

No trial

can deflate us

You are joy to the Nth degree

I can't explain what you've meant to me

As soon as you accepted me

I knew what it was

Not lust not a crush

Naw, this is Grown Folk Love

Sun kissed

Ebony, Bronze, Tan, Brown

Pressing on written JJB

The end of our journey is far within the cave. Why haven't this new generation tilled the road for a new tomorrow? Have the beasts from the future enslaved our minds? Has our fight for freedom been compromised by one or two fools. Is there anyone willing to stand up and be counted for the sake of common folks? There must be one brave being willing to serve willingly for the unforgotten. Is there one person willing to demonstrate a reason why our life is equal in faith and worth? But wait; there comes one brave spirit willing to redeem the faith lost. He embraces hope with his Sword, fighting for the rights of all. It only takes one delicate

flower to spread its seed along the way.

Time written by JJB

Time when the world is filled with demanding expectations, I am solely lost. As time moves forward, we as people have defaulted and surrendered our thoughts of carless whispers of birds with no direction of recourse. Are there any ideas left worth fighting for? Are words just said to combat our camouflage with ourselves? Where have the power of words and motivation gone? Money and greed have power, but they sit on the sideline while fear unleashes the spoils of this wicked, wicked world, deterring the state of the union and replacing hope with fear. **Love is not owed us but simply an opportunity;** it is a pleasure that only a few will obtain and conquer. Peace has no refuge or place if the walls of opportunities have been blocked by silly speculators. Unmask the hidden agenda and capture time. Release it from its prison! There is no refuge, as time lies in space, all alone, untamed, mocking mankind.

We live in fear not by
choice but by
the uncertainities of what
will come

No Regrets Written by Jamey Wilkins

There's too much

Ahead of me

Too many traps

Potholes

Snares

Speed bumps

Strategically placed

To knock me out of the race

I've slipped

Tripped

Fell on my face

But each time

I learned

I Grew

So the next time

I knew

To sidestep

Jump

Slow down

I have to stay alert

To prevent myself

From being hurt

From being attacked

I have no time

Too look back

Change written by JJB

Only one person can change the character of one's fate.

Only one person can fight the battle with a thought.

Only one person can assume the role of a leader.

Facing twisted roads ahead,

Struggling through coils and bumps that lie ahead.

Only I can travel through this single circle.

I am a man written by JJB

Blood bathed in tears, it seems like decades ago. They have walked in the shadows of the ones that had come before me, screaming for fairness, as they roamed the streets, covered in sheets.

They are cowards because they put on a disguise, let them stand as a man for their beliefs without covering up there hate with white sheets. I walk steady and firm because I am who I say I am, **a Man.**

What constitutes a Man, why am I still considered a boy? If I walk like a man, let me be what I am, **a Man.**

Why do you call me out of my name, if I
don't have the strength to work longer hours,
when I am aching and my body is sore?
Why can't I ride my Mercedes along the road,
without being stopped and interrogated for
hours or so?
Why am I considered less of a man because I
dare to challenge the ill fate of my brothers,
who were falsely accused and now live a life
behind bars, for what they truly don't know?
Can't I rest for a while, without people
staring, accompanied with the sound of a
sirens, when I walk out my door
Why can't I move into your neighborhood
without pressure from my friends fearing I am
not who I am
All I ask, all I want, is to be a Man!

Successful Failure written by JW

I wanna make it

I swear I do

But I know I won't

It seems like

Fate won't allow me to

No matter

How hard I try

I fail

No matter

How sincere I am

How determined I am

I just can't get past

My past

Mr. Freeze written by Jamey Wilkins

A mother

No father

A brother

No sister

A daughter

No son

A heart

No love

What a Child Needs written by JJB

Cuddled in a prone position there sit's a young child. The child is not yet an adult but the burden of this world has destroyed her every being. This young child has no one to love or protect her innocence or teach her the value of life's woes. Her life has just begun, yet she has seen more than one child could ever hope to see or conquer in a life time. Then the child sparkles from the corner of her eyes, as a young couple passes by, the couple looks at every feature, every mole, as they write down notes, as if an appraisal was needed. But wait, the young couple retraces their steps, as they both question every detail of the young child existence. Suddenly for no apparent reason, they stop. she wonders is there hope at last? Will she have her own bed, decorated in a flower print with roses in the background with hundreds of pink, brown and yellow teddy bears, filling up her own room, as she sleep at night. Will her night hold happy memories, with both a mother and father? Will she have happy thoughts instead of another day with bitter sorrows? It depends on this young couple, do they want a boy or a girl, it depends on her smile, did it captured them and will it change her entire world? A child needs some support as you see, to protect them from the hollow hole that creeps in their dreams as they sleep.

A child needs loving hands to comfort them

in the midst of pain.

But most of all, a child need comfort in

knowing they have a loving home; a place

where they can learn and grow until they are

grown.

Fragments written by Gidget E. Seaborne

Sitting here going nowhere

What am I to do?

My mind is so overwhelmed.

Fragments of times, places, sites,

Flowing in and out.

What am I to do?

Wondering why I cannot seem to

put a handle on it.

Wondering why I am still here.

Is there a purpose? Is there a hope?

Sitting here going nowhere

What am I to do?

Hope rides on the petticoat

Of Another day

Repercussions written by Jamey L. Wilkins

Motivation

Spurned by education

Inspired by the history

The obstacles, overcome

The hurdles, leapt

The mountains, climbed

The blood, shed

The leaders, dead

Fearless they stood

So intrepid I will stand

Proud, to be a black man

In the Midst of Darkness written by JJB

In the midst of darkness adorned among a pine tree, a vacant plant evolves, overflowing with fruits and colored leaves, as the light shines from heaven, it seems swallowed by the sun beauty. The frogs and the grasshoppers flee to the forest, as the hunters charge on, to hunt and capture the beauty statuette dole, hiding behind the trees. The moment is still, only silence remains, and then there is a drop of dew, smothering through the rain. The hours are winding down, it is about time to go, but the moment of pleasure is still amongst us and the excitement is more than a person can score. The forest is entrenched with such marvel; evergreens from

sight to sight.. A landscape impressive by far,

a enchanted place filled with dreams

It help me scope amidst the darkness, in a world filled with

beauty and peace.

Family

The thread that ties us by blood

_____

Being in Love written by JJB

This is my testimony of love, from morning, noon, and night. My thoughts are entwined with raw emotions; as I remembered the pleasure of your hands, gently touching my flesh, powerless to move for fear this special moment would end. Mesmerized by your voice, I became overwhelmed with a tingling sensation. Consumed with your charisma, my heart increased its rhythm with every glance in my direction. Only you have the power to control this rhythm. My life has no meaning without the warm fragrance of your body. How can I soften the illusion of my heart without causing this aroma to dissolve? I gave you too much authority, the authority to make me happy. Only a fool will give up such an endowment. Please give me my life back, because I lost it, when I fell so madly and deeply in Love.

The sun shines not because of our works but because of he that created thee

———————————

Heir written by Jamey Wilkins

My feet hurt

And I've not taken one step

My back aches

And I've not received one lash

My heart is broken

And I've not yet loved

How can this be?

Because pain is hereditary

I remembered

She smiled when she gave me a bath, only a

baby, but nevertheless a child.

Gazing up at her loving eyes, I smiled.

My first walk, I wiggled and wobbled, she

guided me with both hands with a smile.

My first words, "DaDa,"

But she took no offense, she picked me up

and kissed me lovingly on my cheeks.

My first day at school, when she had to leave,

I cried out a loud scream because fear was in

my eyes; she nervously gave me to my

teacher; staring backward with an uneasy

smile. When I felt pain from a hurt, she gave

me a hug with loving arms, saying "It's all right my beautiful child."

I looked at her; this time it was me who smiled. The day of my graduation, my heart was beating faster than a mile, but when I looked out in the audience, there proudly taking pictures was my mom, looking at me with a heartfelt smile.

Now, I'm grown and I have a child.

I hope I can be half the woman my mother was to me; looking down at my daughter, I'm so proud to be a mom; it' a pleasure watching my little girl smile.

Ghetto Language written by Jamey Wilkins

I communicate

More effectively

With my fists

I can only seem

To get my point across

With sharp objects

I am better understood

More clearly heard

When a trigger is pulled

I've learned violence

Is a motivational speaker, while peace

Is a boring monotone

If I ask politely I am ignored, If I beg I am scorned

If I say nothing I am oppressed

If I curse…

I am paid attention to

Power to do what you say by JJB

How many piles of wood do I have to chop and stockpile?

Before the marauder realize that *I'm a force of nature* that can't be rechained or demonized.

How many more bridges do I have to jump and avoid, before the chaser realize that this goal in my heart was meant to be nurtured, the day I was born.

To be able to walk this path and retrace another day, I petitioned the counterfeiters to stay out of my way.

If people only realize that life, don't *owe them a thing.*

Life only waits until maturity to claim the fame and tally the score, then it's a game of chance if you want more.

Chin up and seek other directions!

Maturity takes time, sometimes it's a waiting game. But if you choose your path wisely and control your speech,

You will gain control whenever you speak.

The Essence of Fear written by Jamey Wilkins

Trying to hurry home, walking up the street at night

Then all of a sudden you hear footsteps coming behind you.

Glance over your shoulder

But you cannot pick up a trace of anyone

Walk faster

It seems as if the footsteps pick up the pace and begin to run

You start trotting

But it seems like they're galloping

You're hollering

Turn around and nobody's following

Heart racing, you finally make it to your door step

Whew! It's over

Then somebody taps you on your shoulder!

Helpless written by Jamey Wilkins

I converse with the deaf

But I don't think they hearing me

Explained my problems to a paraplegic

But I don't think he feeling me

I traveled with the lame

But they don't keep up

I tried to listen to a mute

But he won't speak up

I'm stuck

What did I do to make them treat me this way?

That is how I feel

when people expect more from me

than I am able to give.

Who Are You by Jamey Wilkins

I thought I knew you

I honestly believed you listened, and understood me

But you were only looking for contradictions

You smile

But for some strange reason it resembles a sneer

Who are you?

I wonder sometimes if your motives are sincere

My true friend

I considered the bond we share as sacred

How can such a lovely façade conceal so much hatred?

Who are you? As I look closer I think I finally see who you are

You are a reflection of me

Priceless memories written by Jamey Wilkins

Traveling backwards

Helps me move forward

Surviving the present

By living in the past

Remembering the golden days

I wonder what happened

Was it simply fool's gold?

That turned my neck green

Was I just transfixed?

By the beautiful gleam

Nah, it was 24 karat

It just got stolen

And replaced

With a worthless fake

But I can't discard it, because it is all I have

To remind me of how it use to be

What Counts written by Jamey Wilkins

You know I love you right?

If you don't I apologize

For not allowing my actions

To express the feelings I have inside

Maybe I haven't tried

But I thought I did

And isn't it the thought that counts?

I'll be There written by JLW

I may procrastinate

I may hesitate

But I will never break

My stride

Cause I am never fake

Just to set it straight

In case you thought

I lied

You can set a date

I may be late

But you can bet ya fate

On one thing

If you set and wait

Til the stress abate

One of these days

I'm coming!

True Lies written by Jamey Wilkins

What the majority perceives

To be true

Is what the majority believes

Even if it's a lie

Wisdom prevails

Where ignorance fails

But you cannot fail

If you never try.

Senseless written by Jamey Wilkins

Through the eyes of a man

Through the eyes of a girl

Through the eyes of a nut

In the eyes of a squirrel

Through the eyes of a snail

As it slides through the world

From the eyes of a rock

That's disguised as a pearl

With the ears of a bat

I can hear where you at

I can sense when you tense

Like a hound with no scents

Aimless

A gun with no barrel

Stainless
Still, I feel, it's painless

Probably written by JLW

Have you lost the ability

To show your sensitivity?

Have all your emotions

Been worn away by erosion?

Have you become automation?

Answering questions how you ought to respond?

Asking things like, "How you doing?"

When you don't give a damn how he doing

You're probably foul

When things go wrong
Sarcastically, you probably smile

If the answer to any of these questions was yes

You're probably a mess

You're probably depressed.

Taste and See written by Geraldine Jenkins

Taste the sweet honey drops on the flowers

Lovely adorned with feathers designed like insects

This scenery is forever printed in my memories

When memories of changes have withered, our love will never fade

Flowers bloom, as seasons change

Let us taste and see this beauty.

Progress Onward by Geraldine Jenkins

Mountain bound toward the peak of his career, frail but he climb on,

He stepped on all the noses and toes of family and friends to progress

toward his goal. But he fails to rest, inch by inch, he climbed the ladder to success; his riches undefined. Once there he met the chill side of the test for his success.

The mission for success corrupted his mind that finally killed his body that laid gently in the parlor. There was no one to mourn or cry because he stepped on all the nice people along the way; the ones who truly cared.

Love found by Geraldine Jenkins

Why is my heart longing?

To love, as noon rises above the heart, it

means you are in love.

Many seas away in the Blue Moon, in a

distance place afar from the dwelling of the

lonely heart, love surge beyond the sweet rage

of old father time.

With waves of passion, trembling, conquering

the hope of endless restless time.

I sit lonely, waiting to find a willing heart that

will ease my pain to stop my bleeding heart. It

might come as a shadow, it might come

before day but I will sit by my window and

wait, hoping I will see his face.

Respect written by Jamey Wilkins

As we stroll I focus my eyes on her

Inattentive to skimpy attire, as temptation walks by

I erase negative connotations, degrading her being

Remove expletives from my vocabulary flirtatious actions diminish.

Blown away with the wind

A grin replaces anger

A violent force never touches her soul

Untold is the story of respect

Extinct in repulsive ways

My grandmother, my sister

My mother, my aunt

My wife, my daughter

Demand it

Respect those who enabled you to be

They deserve it!

Through the Eyes of the Warrior
written by Jamey L. Wilkins

Victory is so elusive

Nearly impossible to get a good aim on it

I give chase, but whether I trot or gallop

I still never seem to gain on it

I'm weary, I'm weak, I'm tired

It hurts to take each and every breath

Yet I tell myself "only one more to go"

After each and every step

Odds against me it seems hopeless

Wounded from a near kill

By law my body should've collapsed

Yet it operates off of shear will

There are too many hopes and dreams

Placed on my fragile shoulders

But it's a weight I gladly bear

For it is the plight of a true soldier

If I don't stand, who will?

When it is clear that someone must

That's why trudge on relentlessly

After victory's scent from dawn til dusk

I cannot fail, I will not fail

I know it can be done

Even if I don't achieve it myself

This battle can be won.

So victory, you may as well submit

Through I'm no follower or leader

What makes me a warrior?

Is simply that I'm a believer

Being a Man Written by Earnest Jenkins

Look around you and see

At the beginning of time

Do you see yourself as a man?

But yet you cannot stand alone

You tried so hard to impress other

"Be a man"

Look around you

At the beginning of time

You were born to win

but you decided to fail

You became the Man!

Look around you! the world is not so pretty now

Someone realized that you were a winner but you gave up

Who are you?

Web of Lies written by JJB

My body is woven down in a web of deceit

Why does the truth ridicules me? I try to tell the truth

But society wants to hear a lie

I say to you my friend; I'm honest, while descending into a web of deceit

My flesh is beaten down; I hunger for remorse but my mind is feeble.

Questioning myself, I ask, is there any exquisite delight in the truth?

How can I trust my integrity when it speaks falsehood, a commonality that I've lost along the way.

My speech is twisted, as the web of lies swallows my tongue

I am caught up in a world of trickery but wait; I will be honest and speak

There is no truth unless there are others around to hear me speak, so I will remain quiet.

How can I overcome the hardships this world offers because the truth is unheard of?

My web of lies have destroyed my integrity as I attempt to compose myself, as the

Sun set in the blazing heat of the day, I will try my best to murmur the truth out, before it gets caught up in my web of lies.

Wisdom written by Gidget E. Seaborne

She struts like a queen."

She is phenomenal.

She is my teacher.

One who exceeds excellence

One who has strengths beyond my comprehension.

One who reaches for and obtains the untouchable.

One who is wise beyond her years.

One who I learn from

I marvel at her insight.

She is phenomenal.

She is my teacher.

To Know written by Jamey Wilkins

That is all I ever wanted. No amount of money or material possession can compare to this intangible ability. As I look back on my life I realize that if I had only known my life would have turned out different. If I had known that, even though it looked cool, associating with thugs, gangsters and drug dealers I would be considered one, even though I was neither…

If I had known that being in their presence I would unconsciously pick up some of their bad characteristics such as, being disrespectful to my elders, smoking and drinking which would further tarnish my image and creditability…..

If I had known that school was a blessing instead of a burden. That social studies (boring!) actually applied to me, that English would help me communicate more effectively, maybe just maybe I would not be where I am today, incarcerated.

It's funny because during my search to find guns and knives to protect myself from those who I willingly hung around, the most powerful weapon on earth was so easily accessible. More powerful than a machine gun, it even surpasses the strength of a nuclear weapon. The most valuable thing costs absolutely nothing, knowledge. It is something that everyone can possess but no one can truly own.

Yeah, If I had only known…

But hold up, the beauty of knowledge is that it is never too late to acquire it. Your past is just that, your past. It's over with, it can't be changed but it can be converted from a foolish mistake to a humbling lesion. Learn from it, so your future will not be a re-enactment of it.

Education is essential to growth, so if you want to become a grown man, a grown woman, and be considered by others as one, first you must be willing to learn. The foundation of learning is listening: to your parents, your teachers, your conscience, to people who have been down the road you are just now approaching.

If only I had listened I would not have to actually feel fire to know it burned. I would not have to retrace my footsteps to get back where I already was before I made this wrong turn.

If only I had known…..

Knowledge is infinite and unlike money or material things once you use it you still have it. You can learn from everything and everyone in existence, even me.

Everything you ever wanted is within your grasp, all you have to do is reach out and grab it, be it that next book or magazine. Now I know you're thinking who is he, to tell me anything, how does he know." Well, I know because I was once your age, I know because I learned through trial and error, I know because I started to listen. As for who I am…..

Ha! I go by the name Experience.

No Cure written by Jamey Wilkins

Terminally sick

Eternally ill

Yearning a fix

Of infirmary pills

If I had one wish

I 'd wish to be healed

Cause pain is the only

Condition I feel

What did I do

Why am I cursed

When will it end

Why does it hurt

Hoping to live

Anxious to die

Too late to care

Too weak to cry

No turning back

No way to run

It seems I forgot

The meaning of fun

It won't go away

Though I pray and I plead

Inflicted afflicted

With a fatal disease

The Road to Riches written by Jamey Wilkins

Being stripped of it

Made me realize their value

I used to not care

They came a dime a dozen

Now out of a dozen

I can't even get a dime

Never had I risked my heart

I always played it safe

That's the way playas play

But I don't wanna be a playa no more

Cause won't nobody play with me

I'm a grown man now

I have no time for childish games

I want to experience the real thing

Now that I've been broke

I know the beauty the strength

The power a woman possesses

I desperately want to cherish

To adore, to pour out my empty heart

And love her

For only that priceless possession

Can make me rich

This time once she's mine

I'll never let her go

Wasted years written by JJB

Tick, Tock, years turned into decades

Old father time, where have you departed

Reality, seems so far away

Once, I was a voyager, a person without a plan

I'm older now, with no more seeds to sow

Times are hard, words of literacy foreign to me

As the sweat falls off my face, I seek redemption.

For years, my weakness slaved me and seduced me into a coma like state

There is hope I say, hope that my life has some decree

Bitterness swells inside of me as my soul cries out for succor

Tears only for the silent years, the time when I was trying to find my way

I spent years climbing the corporate ladder while neglecting to enjoy the light of happiness

At last, I see the rainbow hidden behind the clouds

Camouflaged between the clouds, I see blue, red, orange and white

Years wasted or hidden from my sight.

Upbringing written by Jamey Wilkins

Profiled as so wild, uncouth

Young youth

Unaware of where

They came from

Unaware of what

They're made of

Some say they gave up

Blame it on the father

The one who didn't bother

Or maybe the mother

The one who stayed uncovered

Half naked half crazy

Why did she have babies?

Why was she allowed?

Why not?

Who told her she shouldn't

Not you, not me

But the media cause what is portrays

Has turned boys gay

Women into dykes

And they actually believe it's alright

Alright, okay, I give

I'ma let you live

Passivity has birthed

The worse of the worse

What happened to the rod

Who said spare it?

The same people that can afford to

I can't afford not to

So I won't

And please don't

Bring ya wild, uncouth

Young youth

Unaware of where

They came from

Around my sons

Around my daughters because I am a father

Who doesn't care if I bother?

My child or not

They gon' grow up right

Conscious about life

Respectful

And I bet you

They pass it on

One Way by JLW

Once said

Words cannot be taken back

They only travel one way

So when speaking

One must be careful

What one say

The tongue is the road

The voice is the car

The mind is the engine

The oil is the thoughts

That lube up the brain

When designing a sentence

Emotion press the gas

While the conscience controls the brakes

When feelings are at stake, be careful what you say

Because once said words cannot be taken back

They only travel one way

Sins of This World written by JJB

Hypocrisy is the sin of this world

Haughtiness cause people to rise and fall

Furtive as a fox, they lay waiting for any sign of weakness

Pretending to be amiable to appease the situation of the lost

Hatred is brazen on their tongues. Callous thoughts arcane

(secret) hidden

On their pillow at night. Avarice, has destroyed their soul

Why do men and women want more than they are worth

when they speak?

Candor words are often spoken, only to appease the

followers of the unforgotten.

Why do we have to debase the young and the innocent

While the character of the people we love, we decry.

Sarcastically, I laugh. In my demure state my eyes watered.

I am the finest of the fine.

My followers will destroy the weak with their blades.

Where are the fools, the ones that wouldn't open the door

when I needed food, shelter, and wisdom. People scorned me

until there was only a shell of a person left.

Looking in the mirror, I see only a shadow, and in its place

Stood the sins of this world basking in all their glory

Ready and eager to take my place.

You and they written by Earnest Jenkins

I wanted to do things my way. You tried to stop me. They support you in your attempt. I was in charge. You stood in my way. They support you in your stand. You and They came together. I recognized that I could not win. So, I became the you, and they became the I, YOU and THEY

Me Against Me written by Jamey Wilkins

My hand my chest my leg

Things that can be crushed

My love, my knowledge, my fears

Things that can't be touches

My heart my lung my brain

Things that are my physical

My mind my spirit my soul

Things that are invisible

Two components of self

One pulling one pushing

Material and immaterial

One true and one crooked

Constant struggle between me

My heart and my pride

Give or take bend or break

It's hard to decide

Ironic, trying to live

And let neither get the best of me

Catch 22 cause either one I pick

Will eventually be the death of me.

Sometimes remaining silent
Is the best remedy"

Lone Wolf written by Jamey Wilkins

Hatred, jealousy, envy

Manifests themselves in me

So I erupt

Spewing volcanic acid at bastards

Lies, threats to kill them afterwards

Can't put my hands on them

So I assassinate their character

But when all is "said and done."

When all of them are gone

I find I still have those traits

In me when I'm all alone

Real written by Jamey Wilkins

To me

Real doesn't exist

When everyone

Can look at the same thing

And see different

Real is an illusion

It's not a lie

But it's not the truth

For it can't be proven

I can't tell you\

What you see

Neither can you tell me what I

All we can do

Is look in the same direction

And hope the reality

Doesn't pass us by

Me and You, You and me written by Jamey Wilkins

If you could see thru my eyes

I wonder how you would deal with

The pain I hold inside

I wonder if you would look at you

The way I look at you

And if as me you would do

Things I wouldn't do

Then I wonder why

…Hmmm let me try

To look thru your eyes

And see if I would cry

Probably so

But only if I were you

Because then I could do things

That I wouldn't see

Yet we both see the same

How? Well let me explain
To you I'm a disappointment
If you think that that's a lie
You'd be deceiving yourself
Cause I can see it in your eyes
That I didn't achieve
What you know I could achieve
If only I had believed
What you know I should believe
Have considered that
I'm only being myself
And that you see more in me
Than I see in myself
To me you are a disappointment
If you wish that that's lie
You'd be deceiving yourself
Can't you see it in my eyes?
That I expect so much from you
Things I know you can achieve

But you don't want to know

You only want to believe

Maybe I should consider

That you're just being yourself

Do I see more in you

Than you see in yourself

Now do you see how we see

The same but differently

I see what is but you see

What you wish it would be

Have you ever just sat back

And listened to me

And understood what I said

Paid attention to me

I know, I know, true

I never listened to you

So who am I to question

Some of the shit that you do

Remember you said

I have book sense but no common sense

Where I see rare pennies

You only see common cents

I feel you are ashamed of me

And deep down that anger me

Why not accept me for me

And not be intent on changing me

I'll never be ashamed of you

And don't think I'm blaming you

Actually I'm blaming me

For not being what I claim to be

But you are me, I am you

We are one, we are two

When I let you see thru me

I would like to see thru you

Even though I'm gone away

My heart still pumps your blood

If you took the blood away

My heart'd still want ya love

Lovers of the Flesh by JJB

Lovers of the utmost qualities

Passion drove me to overlook what ever

Boundaries there were, yes!

Desires of the flesh conquered all my doubts

Was I a lover in the moment, awe! With raging desires, let me think.

Finally, I was caressed, after years of absentee and empty beds

Now my flesh is warm from the body of my lover

Will this passion last forever?

Who knows?

But for today, my cup is filled from the thirst of his kisses.

A mother plead to child to be strong written by JJB

Momma, momma, I can't!

Child speak out! Tell them they are wrong!

But momma, I can't!

Be strong my child!

But momma, what will happen if I protest?

Honey, the hour is near; our burdens must be cast out.

We must rise out from the ashes to voice our troubles, there are no more slaves.

What do you mean momma?

To let things stay the same denotes not being a part of the change.

Oh, oh

So, if I'm calm, if my contemplation goes unheard, there will be no change.

No, my child.

Then I must rise up from the fear that common man/woman bounds me

Momma, do you think I can ever conquer my fear, to challenge the wrongs?

Yes! My child

Because you represent the future of all men/women

It is the hope that closes or opens each door

You are the future that bounds men/women accountable to their own deeds

To live in Peace written by JJB

Peace, this word, few get the preference to enjoy, Life, broken by hunger and pain. Neighbors or foes, it seems that life is a game. Are we destined by our animal instinct, to be a wild beast or a prey! Do we want to die from the knife that probes our backs from the shadows of our so-called friends, or to live in peace? It's 'an opportunity that we all must search for, it's a decree that we all must abide by. It's a dream that we all must cherish and uphold, it's the factual knowledge that distinguish us from the wild animals of the prey or the man/woman that walks the street on their excursion to find peace.

To live

To pray, to die in Peace!

Love doesn't happen by Chance by JJB

We smiled

We danced

We enlightened each other about our thoughts

I'm in love

L-O-V-E

No time to waste

Gotta get married!

Um

Such a fool,

Instant romance

Means, instant Pain

Love doesn't happen by chance

Love is a reality that feeds the heart.

What does the word Friend means? By JJB

Rugged roads I faced, struggling to find my place

But I made it, did you my black friend help me, ah, ah

Please! I begged! Can you buy this, can you at least help me with

My flyers, my promotions, after all, it's your area of expertise

Call me back later, you stated!

Tried to bring about awareness about my passion, negativity, what're

you doing that for! Bluntly, you stated.

Aren't we inspired to be good citizens, to go after the American Dream?

We as Blacks have long forgotten the plights that our forefathers have

Fought so hard for

The right to unite, the right to come together, to solicit a bond that

excite and unify

But we have become so attuned to the way things are

We are lazy when it comes to fighting for causes that affect us all

We expect others to fight our battle while we sat and watch, sipping

Beers or sodas at night

Then we cry for justice when it hits home

Well, you did nothing!

Now, you are another black person gone.

Why should I help you now, my hands are tied

Your mouth was foreign from my ears when I needed you

I needed a confidant

But I made it, so I'm returning the errand, if you had asked, if you

had simply cared about me, my accomplishments wouldn't even mattered

The burden of prove, Awe, there wouldn't been an argument, in your case

But some say, "a tooth for a tooth"

My dear friend

But I'm not made from the same cloth, if we can't forgive, we will never grow

Ah, I will see what I can do

Let me be for real

Today is a new day, if we pull together and not

act beyond our means because we are the same, not by the segregated

factors that surrounds our life but by common factors that connect us

my dear friend

Africa We Hear Your Cry written by JJB

Trouble placed on the burden of a nation but many Countries have passed you by. Many sit in silence, with thoughts of unbelief, emotionless to the call. These people are hurting! They are starving and dying.

We see picture of kids starving, endemic enclaves their stomach, violence in every aspect of their life. There are massacres disguised in all forms, bleeding their minds of the property of life. A Child's innocence is lost every day among the bully breast, leaving them hopeless, wounded by different priority at best. It takes more than a wonder or just a How do you do. No one person can do it all. It takes thousands or even millions to answer the call. The call to educate people so they lend a hand, we all should help fight this plight. We can't remove our conscious and say it is not our cause.

"Check yourself before you judge someone else"

A Boy Named Nigger written by Jamey Wilkins

They call me ignorant

They call me insane

They call me everything

Except by my name

I'm looked down on, frowned on

Old folks hate to say it

When they see me

They just shake their head

A lost cause

I am not what they wanted me to be

I don't follow rules I don't agree with

I am free, they can't see. Why I don't submit

Why I endure punishment

Why I won't quit! I have to be crazy

Blame it on my father. The one I never knew

The one that never bothered to teach me

"If love is causing you pain, well, it'nt love"

"Don't assume the worse from others! Take a blind step of faith and assume nothing"

Paying your dues

Insight in writing this piece was, so many times we value materialistic things instead of honoring God sometimes we forget that his mercy allows us to be and strive.

When I write, I try to base my thoughts on these themes: "A time to live, rejoice, cry, and a time to die." These are my premises in which I cultivated my inspirations.

Even though, our choices are no joking matter, the author adds humor with a twist.

Paying my dues written by JJB

Paying my dues were easy on earth, now I must wait at the pearly gates to see if it were enough? The pastor preached a good sermon but was it enough to make up for my life on earth? Boy, wasn't that sermon good? it almost made me want to get up and walk out. But I didn't see any tears shed. The building was sparcely packed or was there a lot of people? I can't remember. Where were all my family members? Were they in the other room? I can't remember! Where was the lady down the street with that beautiful purple hat? Oh, did I forget to tell her, "Hi" when her husband lost his job? I hurried past her because I didn't want to hear her beg. Can't remember, Can't remember. With money, there is fame, maybe I will buy my way to heaven. Let me see, I'm riding my Mercedes in the pearly gates now, Aint my ride fine? It was easy living on Earth without a care, because money made things happen. There was no time to comfort my neighbors, no time to say hey. The Bible, you got to be kidding! I didn't have time for that! It was work as usual, reading the Bible would have been time consuming. Please pass me a glass of wine so I can chill! My day at work was tiresome as always. Busy as a bee, no time to treat anyone with kind words. But I had time for my money and the luxury it offered. It was worth more than a Hi or The Bible. But this road is so wide, people have so much room. But why are they not speaking? Why do they look so sad? The road ahead seems even gloomier. There is a hollow look on all the people's faces, where are we going I asked? Everyone stopped and looked back at me. "Look around you, they said." "Do the people look happy?" "No! I replied." "Well you know now, all your life' you built your fortune, never giving God any time, the path you've chosen was the wrong one. Now you are on the road with the lost souls, there will be a judgment.

You tried to buy yourself into Heaven, being silly, riding your Mercedes trying to get into the pearly gates.

Most of us weren't that dumb! We rode our bikes attempting to look humble. Then you tried to write a check and guess what? Your money was returned, no address for worldly goods. But, but, I have money

Everyone looked back, "we're too sad to laugh but you just baked the cake."

All your time you spent honoring your worldly possessions, do you honestly think God gonna find favor in you?

Get back in the back of the line!

Stop smiling you clown! Where do you think you going?

Insight pages from author's point of view

- We must hold people accountable for their Wrongdoings.
- Gun violence, it affects us all.
- Racist exist but we can't let it stop our progress.
- When I see and hear that someone has been gunned down for simple driving a car, or being profiled for no other than the color of their skin, it hurts.
- When I hear of mass shooting at schools, my heart grieves for their love ones's pain.

- Even though, we don't see their truths, the Bible plainly says "You reap what you sow"
- The rule of law should apply to all!

Whatever Platform you use, use it wisely!

Black Man by Earnest Jenkins

The man I am as African American man, is a

strong man.

Will I remain the same as I am?

I was born to an injust world that don't want

to change

They tried to limit my expectations but I

refused to be chained because I am

who I am, a strong Black man

In time I will grow and change , but never

will I forget who I am

Many years will pass by, but will I continue to

accept the man I am

Will I blame the world for the man I have

become

As each day passes and new experiences

happen

Will these new experiences change the man

inside me?

As the sun rises and the sun sets, I will always

be the man that God made me to be

I am what I am, a Man

An Angel in Waiting by JJB

Who was my brother?

Was he a man without flaws?

No because he wasn't perfect, but he

was the kindness and sweetest person I've

ever known.

Whatever flaws he had they were

minus, it seemed to me that he was an angel

in waiting the minute he was born

He had a presence that welcomed you

regardless of your background.

Have you ever seen a person that had

a presence that was extraordinary, something

that can't be described.

If I painted you a picture of how he

was , would you believe me?

To his family, he was an angel in waiting, because his spirit continues to live on in all our hearts.

I remember his wit, I remember his gentleness and most of all, his laughter.

He had what people today called the It factor, but whatever he had, he had it with his loving smile

He was very artistic, his artworks were breath-takingly beautiful; you could see his designs throughout his home, a couple of his paintings were distributed on his job.

Who was this person, we called uncle, brother, father, son and friend?

How can you describe a person whose sole purpose in life was living not for himself but for the One who created him in his likeness and in complete harmony

with his vision

But he is gone now, only for a short

while

He was born from the flesh of a

woman

A father he respected in the midst of

his wrongs. But, nevertheless, he loved him

because he was a loving son.

When I get lonely, I think about my

brother, a breeze breezing by that wrap me up

in his arms saying "my dear sister please be

strong!"

But in that same breath, my brother

was gone.

He was an angel in waiting

in the midst of the darkness he ministered to others when he was sick and in pain not thinking about himself. His life's journey speaks his works because today, in the shadow of our hearts, we are still grieving this heartfelt love .

But the day he passed, all things ceased in their tracks, the day my brother left with no rain check.

But I thank God for his mercy

And his grace, hopefully one day, I will see my brother again

He was an angel in waiting

No regrets by JJB

Yesterday, I gave him all his flowers

Today, I'm at peace

Wordless, I sat and pondered

There are so many things, I wished I

had addressed.

Even though we had our differences,

He brought out my best

Although, I said it so many times,

utterance from my mouth was not enough.

It's the everyday things we sometimes

take for granted

like seeing the person's face or calling

to say hey

No words can replace what I truly feel

But God is a loving God, if we cultivate his teachings by watering our knowledge, our faith will definitely grow.

The Game changing by Earnest Jenkins

It is time to move on

If we see the sun today

We are blessed

If we see the moon tonight

We live for another night

Time can be on our side

But the game changing moment lives in our

life forever

What day is it?

I really don't know

Searching for endless moments

To live or die

In a world of confusion

We are always searching for that moment

The moment or time, we can be what we

want to be

But the questions lie in our heart

That determines what our responses will be

Envisioning Rosa Parks

I wrote this piece envisioning the night before Rosa Parks got on the bus. These are my thoughts about the suspense leading up to this heroic feat. I am trying to bring light to what was going through Rosa's mind the night before the famous stand for freedom. Even though I was not in Rosa's predicament, I used my imagination to convey the significance of what was about to happen. Can you imagine being in this woman's shoes for a second?

After years of planting the seeds of despair, saying that Blacks are heathens, and less than animals, this form of brainwashing takes years to undo. This struggle will not end overnight, but we must start a new day supporting each other by forging new ideas.

We must use whatever platform we have to inform because we as a people have yet to overcome.

Envisioning Rosa Parks before she got on the Bus

The night before she rode the bus

I envision fear embraced Rosa Parks because she was only human, but, she knew emancipation was worth dying for. Would she reach her destination or not? This time it was crucial that she follow through with her plan and not give up; she probably thought about all the runaway slaves, beaten and killed just for rising up against their master's hands. When she took her daily walks, she saw hatred everywhere, signs saying, Coloreds not allowed. This inhumane treatment of black folks, she couldn't understand why it was ever allowed.

I imagine she thought about all the slaves and what they went through, while providing nutrition to their masters's children.

Rosa was probably overwhelmed with thoughts, but she believed in the Power of God.

I imagine Rosa questioned, why did the color of her skin excite misperceptions? She probably thought about all the things she had endured and why it was so relevant that she now make her move.

I envision Rosa weighing her options on whether it was worth the risk of losing everything she had worked so hard to get.

I envision her finally coming to the decision that she couldn't lose something she never had.

Nevertheless, the night before, Rosa probably couldn't get any sleep. What if she had failed to take a stand and the cycle of injustice kept tilting the scale? She probably thought about her husband, would he be saddened by her actions? I imagine she was scared , what if she got beaten or lynched. These are some of the questions I envision she asked herself in the wee hours of the night. The next morning, she probably kneeled down and did another heartfelt prayer. She knew that the power of God was greater than what men could do to her flesh. She probably could feel God's Holy Spirit preparing her for this task, but most of all she had confidence that this mission was about to be won because she believed in the power of prayer. When everything fails, God is always there.

I envision she put on her glasses, took her Bible from her purse and took a deep breath and proceeded to go to work. After working her shift, she waited and waited until
she saw the Bus. Armed with her Bible, this brave soul stepped on the bus

No longer a slave, but a daughter so that made her an heir because after her there would be others taking up the reigns forging their way on the path too freedom while lifting up their eyes and seeing the glory of God.

.

When They Say I'm not who I am

by JJB

When they say I'm not worth a grain of salt, I ask why? Then I reply, aint I the product of Adam and the woman called Eve, the mother of all men and the reigning Queen of sin. The promise fell from grace but was renewed when the Prince of Peace shed his blood as a ranson for the debt that needed to be paid. When they say how are we kin? You are black and I'm white. I laughed and shook my head; I see God's mercy every day, it didn't happen by chance that I woke up this morning with the strength to get out of my bed. Everything that mankind has is in Jehovah's sight

Men have tried to produce life but fail. Why? Because men can't produce life from a tube, that's why all attempts have failed. Adam and Eve had the prospect of living in paradise, but the enemy due to his jealousy had a plan to receive all the glory owed to God, robbing the couple of their place in paradise. Was mankind doom before Adam could produce a seed? No! Because of God's love, he allowed man to be. Our Heavenly Father has mercy, he opened a path for redemption; his Son, the reigning Prince of Prince, Christ Jesus. When Christ Jesus went back to Heaven, he battled the enemy in Heaven and won; casting the enemy down to Earth, now woe to the Earth, because we are on National alert! The enemy knows he has a short time, that's why he is on a mission "to devour and destroy" God is who he say He is, because I believe, and when I look around, his love is all I see. He is "the beginning to no ending." When they say to me"who is he?" I say, he is Jehovah God there is no other like he.

Friends

She was my friend; her hair was straight and my hair was curly. We laughed and played when we were together; she was who she was and that was alright. We never viewed ourselves as being different, even though, I was black and she was white. When we went to school, neither one of us could understand, but we were bessies not letting our challenges affect us being friends. Sometimes she would cry and say "I'm sorry my friend, why do they hate you so? You are just like me but only you have darker skin. Then I would say "that's alright, with your shoulder to lean on, we will fight this until the end." But my white friend got sick and moved away, I forgot to tell her that I loved her dearly, because she instilled in me hope when crying was the only way. She would say, "if you let them win, what would you have to fight for," hate isn't a part of God plan." She lifted me up when people called me names; she would say " how can they love God when they're so filled with rage for a little black girl with pig-tail that is my friend that loves people no matter what their race. I remembered one time, she stood in the way to avoid me getting a hit; this caused a disturbances causing people to walk away and say "stay out of it, you have privileges because of your white skin." Who would dare hit a little blond hair, blue eyed white girl with cherry ribbons with money and authority, it would be suicide to hit this little white girl but if you were black, it would be on, and your ribbons would be in the street. My friend was beautiful, even though she said she never saw anyone as beautiful as me, but nevertheless, she was my bessie that helped steered me from the streets. What was I to do since my friend is gone? But I remembered what my friend said

" Don't you worry your little head a bit, you are the best friend I ever had, my beautiful black friend.

Why do they have to label you?

We are the same, same blood, same mother and same God!

In my books, I try to enlighten people by showing that we are not alone, God put people in our path to help us ride out the storms.

For instance, sometimes we don't know how something happen because it seemed so unreal then someone steps in our path and help guide us toward a better space.

Note pages

Sometimes we can miss

our blessings by

complaining about

things we don't have

Lifting people up elevate

you even higher

www.ingramcontent.com/pod-product-compliance
Lightning Source LLC
Chambersburg PA
CBHW031420290426
44110CB00011B/458